COMMUNICATING
FOR
RESULTS

Rosemary T. Fruehling, Ph.D.
Joan M. Lacombe, M.A., CPS

Devlopmental Editor: Cynthia Miller
Editorial Consultant: Marjorie Lisovskis
Copyeditor: Susan Buie
Text/Cover Designer: Queue Publishing Services Inc.
Desktop Publisher: Christine Gray & Katie Oftedahl
Illustrator: Jorel Williams

ACKNOWLEDGMENTS We wish to thank the following instructors and technical experts who contributed to this book:

Dr. Billie J. Herrin
University of Montana
Missoula, Montana

Ms. Roberta Moore
Consultant
New York, New York

Ms. Carol McGonagill
Pierce College
Auburn, Washington

Ms. Karol Carstensen
Consultant
Minneapolis, Minnesota

Ms. Charlotte Donabedian
Johnson & Wales University
Providence, Rhode Island

Mr. Joseph Tinervia
Consultant
Rahway, New Jersey

Library of Congress Cataloging in Publication Data
Fruehling, Rosemary T.
    Communicating for results / Rosemary T. Fruehling, Joan LaCombe.
        p. cm.
    Includes index.
    ISBN 1-56118-363-6
    1. Communication in management. I. LaCombe, Joan. II. Title.
    HD30.3.F78   1996
    658.4'5--dc20 95-16235   CIP

© 1996 by Paradigm Publishing Inc.
Published by: EMC/Paradigm
                   300 York Ave.
                   St. Paul, MN 55101
                   800-535-6865

Printed in the United States of America

10 9 8 7 6 5 4 3 2 1

CONTENTS

UNIT II   LISTENING FOR RESULTS

UNIT III   SPEAKING FOR RESULTS